SimplyHealthful

PASTA SALADS

THE SIMPLY HEALTHFUL SERIES

Simply Healthful Pasta Salads by Andrea Chesman
Simply Healthful Fish by David Ricketts and Susan McQuillan
Simply Healthful Cakes by Donna Deane and Minnie Bernardino

Simply Healthful

PASTA SALADS

Delicious New Low-Fat Recipes

By Andrea Chesman
Photography by Ernie Sparks

CHAPTERS™

CHAPTERS PUBLISHING LTD., SHELBURNE, VERMONT 05482

Published by
Chapters Publishing Ltd.
2031 Shelburne Road
Shelburne, Vermont 05482

Library of Congress Cataloguing-in-Publication Data

Chesman, Andrea.
Simply healthful pasta salads / by Andrea Chesman;
photography by Ernie Sparks.
p. cm. -- (Simply healthful series)
Includes index.
ISBN 1-881527-06-9 : $9.95
1. Cookery (Pasta) 2. Salads. I. Title. II. Series.
TX809.M17C49 1993
641.8'22--dc20
92-39973
CIP

Trade distribution by
Firefly Books Ltd.
250 Sparks Avenue
Willowdale, Ontario
Canada M2H 2S4

Printed and bound in Canada by
Friesen Printers
Altona, Manitoba

Designed by Hans Teensma/Impress, Inc.

Gold-rimmed platter courtesy of La Cache, Kingston, Ontario
Marble courtesy of Spada Tile Inc., Kingston, Ontario

Contents

Introduction

I USED TO MAKE pasta salads by drenching a bowl of pasta and vegetables with olive oil, then seasoning it with a handful of chopped herbs, a squeeze of lemon and a sprinkling of salt and pepper. The salads were delicious. Unfortunately, they were also high in fat, and eventually it began to seem silly to take such an inherently healthful dish and drown it in oil.

If you want to make a pasta salad that is both low in fat *and* delicious, you can't just reduce the amount of oil or replace it entirely with lemon juice and vinegar. For one thing, without the oil to coat the strands, the pasta will absorb all the dressing and taste dry. For another, adding too much acid in the form of lemon juice or vinegar will upset the balance of flavors.

As I experimented with reducing the amount of oil, I picked up a few tricks that enabled me to create pasta salads that are as moist and satisfying as those with higher levels of fat. In most salads, I coat the pasta with some oil—up to a tablespoon—to "seal" the pasta before adding the dressing. That way, I can use less dressing for more flavor. Adding a cup or so of chopped fresh parsley—or another herb—to a dressing helps it cling to the pasta better.

Several low-fat ingredients can add moisture to salad dressings in lieu of lots of oil. Defatted chicken broth is a marvelous extender for vinaigrettes. Its rich flavor enhances the dressing. V8 juice or tomato juice can stretch a spicy or herbal dressing, while white grape juice works well for salads that contain fruit.

If you are sensitive to sodium, you should season carefully. Most of these recipes call for salt to taste. Judiciously used, salt greatly enhances a recipe. In particular, pasta should be cooked in salted water—at least a tablespoon per gallon of water. Keep in mind that those recipes that use soy sauce or fish sauce as a flavoring base tend to be higher in sodium than other recipes.

With a little extra effort, you can make a salad that is as attractive as it is healthful. Take care to match the size and shape of the vegetables with the pasta, and pay attention to color combinations. Red bell peppers or green peas often add the splash of contrast needed. Many vegetables—asparagus, broccoli, green beans, zucchini—have brighter color and better flavor after they have been briefly blanched. Blanching does take an extra step, as well as an extra pot, but it is worth it.

Toss the pasta gently to avoid breaking it up. (Wagon wheels are particularly vulnerable.) Overcooked pasta is also more fragile, so time it carefully.

Most of the salads look best in a dark glazed or clear glass bowl that is wide and shallow. When serving individual portions, I like to nest the salad in a bed of greens—generally watercress, arugula and other sharp-tasting ones.

Most pasta salads are at their best when first made. If you have to prepare one early in the day, it's a good idea to combine all the ingredients for the salad in a mixing bowl, cover tightly and refrigerate. Then combine all the dressing ingredients in a separate jar; cover and refrigerate. The salad and dressing will keep well for up to a day this way. Before serving, let both return to room temperature, if possible. Remix the dressing with a whisk, pour over the salad and toss. Transfer to a serving bowl and garnish as directed.

Leftover pasta salads, however, will need a little doctoring to restore their brightness of flavor. A squeeze of fresh lemon juice and/or a drizzle of chicken broth should do the trick for most. If the dressing is a creamy one, moisten it with additional buttermilk. If fresh herbs are called for, sprinkling in a little more will do wonders for reviving the taste the second time around. You may want to adjust other seasonings as well—adding a little salt and pepper, a dab of mustard or vinegar—to bring the salad back. Don't forget that it will have more flavor at room temperature than it will straight out of the refrigerator.

The recipes that follow are designed to be quick and easy. For most, by the time the pasta has cooked, the other ingredients will be ready and the salad can be assembled. Most use readily available ingredients that can be found without special shopping trips. By the way, many of the dressings in this book are also as delicious on green salads as they are on pasta salads, which is why the ingredients for the dressings are often separated from the salad ingredients.

These salads serve 6 generously as an appetizer or side dish, or 4 generously as a main dish, with only a loaf of bread needed to complete the meal. On a buffet table, figure on 8 to 12 servings per recipe.

———————

The salads contain a maximum of 30 percent of calories from fat, with fewer than 20 grams of fat per serving.

The following guidelines were used in determining the analysis:

- When a recipe offers a choice within the ingredient list, the first ingredient listed is the one represented in the recipe analysis.
- When an ingredient is listed as "optional," it is not included in the analysis.
- Ingredients added "to taste" are not included in the analysis.
- When a range of serving sizes is given, the recipe is analyzed for the larger portion: If it "Makes 4 to 6 servings," it is analyzed for 4 servings.

Pasta Primer

ITALIAN PASTAS

Bowties: A small pasta shaped like bowties.

Cavatelli: Medium-size shells with ruffled edges. A good shape for holding dressing and diced ingredients.

Farfalle: "Butterflies." Medium-size pasta shaped like butterflies.

Linguine: Long, flat noodles.

Orzo: Small pasta shaped like grains of rice.

Penne: "Quills." Thin, medium-size tubes with diagonally cut edges.

Radiatore: Rippled, short pasta shapes that look something like radiators or accordions. They hold dressing well.

Shells: Pasta shaped like conch shells (conchiglie). Come in small, medium and large sizes. Good for holding dressing and diced ingredients. A nice shape to underscore a seafood theme.

Tortellini: Small, stuffed pasta bundles.

Twists: Medium-size pasta spirals. Also called twists, spirals or rotini, depending on the manufacturer. Sometimes available in different colors.

Wagon wheels: Medium-size wheel shapes. Also called ruote, rotelle.

Ziti: Medium-size pasta tubes with straight-cut edges.

ORIENTAL NOODLES

Oriental wheat noodles: Made from wheat, and often with egg. Similar to fresh Italian pasta. Can substitute linguine.

Rice sticks: Sparkling white, broad, flat noodles made from rice flour.

Rice vermicelli: Sparkling white, very thin noodles made from rice.

Soba noodles: Japanese noodles made from buckwheat flour. They are taupe-colored, distinctively flavored and chewy in texture.

(See photograph, pages 10–11.)

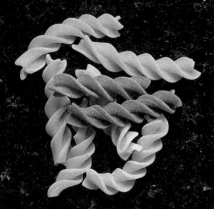

TWISTS

FARFALLE

BOWTIES

WAGON WHEELS

RADIATORE

PENNE

SHELLS

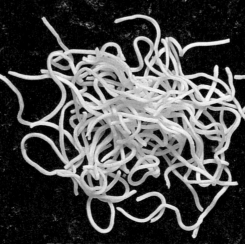

FRESH CHINESE NOODLES

SOBA NOODLES

ORZO

LINGUINE

ZITI

RICE STICKS

RICE VERMICELLI

TORTELLINI

The Pasta Salad Pantry

IF THESE INGREDIENTS are stocked in your cupboards or refrigerator, you should be able to prepare most of the recipes in this book without making a special shopping trip.

Staples

Pasta: Keep an assortment on hand. My favorites for salads are twists, penne, shells, radiatore and orzo. A few of the salads require linguine, but in general, long noodles don't work as well with lighter dressings. For most salads, substitutions are fine. Keep in mind, though, that the salad will be most attractive if the vegetables and pasta are of similar size or shape—diced vegetables go with short or round shapes, julienned vegetables go with long, thin shapes. So if you substitute a different-shaped pasta in a recipe, you may want to adjust the way you chop the vegetables.

For Asian-style salads, I rely on fresh Chinese noodles, which are found in the produce section of most supermarkets. You can substitute ¾ pound of dry linguine for 1 pound of the fresh noodles. I also love to cook with delicate, sparkling-white rice vermicelli, which is found wherever Asian foods are sold. The broader rice sticks may be substituted for rice vermicelli, but no wheat noodle makes an adequate substitute.

Oil: I use extra-virgin olive oil almost exclusively. Its rich, fruity flavor greatly enhances most pasta salads, but you can, of course, use regular olive oil whenever you prefer. For many of the Asian-style recipes, I use dark sesame oil. There is no acceptable substitute for either ingredient.

Vinegar: Red-wine vinegar and balsamic vinegars work well in pasta salads. If you happen to have flavored red-wine vinegars, by all means use them where you think they would be appropriate. Chinese rice-wine vinegar is used in the Asian-style salads. It is a mild, slightly sweet vinegar. If you need a last-minute substitute, use diluted white vinegar to which you have added a pinch of sugar.

Fat-Free Mayonnaise: In general, I prefer to avoid imitation foods—and I find fat-free mayonnaise straight out of the jar to be pretty awful.

I've found that blending fat-free mayonnaise with a little olive oil and a splash of lemon juice improves both taste and texture.

Canned Chicken Broth: You can extend a vinaigrette or pesto with canned chicken broth with excellent results. Shop around for a brand you like (avoid those with hydrolyzed yeast, which imparts a canned-soup flavor). Be sure to skim off the yellow fat that rises to the top of the can. Leftover broth can be refrigerated for a few days—or better yet, freeze leftover broth in ice cube trays and use it to enhance soup stocks and sauces or to steam vegetables. Salads dressed with chicken broth are usually more perishable than those without the broth, so keep them refrigerated.

Roasted Red Peppers: It is useful to have a jar of roasted red peppers on hand. You can substitute them for fresh red peppers; they will add color and flavor to any salad.

If a recipe calls for roasted red peppers and you prefer to roast your own, here's how to do it. Place the peppers in contact with a hot flame—on the burner of your gas stove, under a broiler or on a barbecue—turning frequently, until the skin is bubbly and blackened. Put the peppers in a brown paper bag, seal the top and place in the freezer for about 10 minutes. The peppers should be cool enough to handle and the skins should slip off when you pull them gently and slowly, lifting up with the tip of a paring knife. Rinse the peeled peppers under cold running water.

Capers: These pickled flower buds have a salty essence that pairs beautifully with lemon and seafood. Without their sprightly flavor, many salads would be lackluster and bland.

Garlic and Onions: I use garlic and red onions a lot, as well as chives (snipped from my garden) and scallions.

Soy Sauce, Fish Sauce, Oyster Sauce: These sauces, found wherever Asian foods are sold, flavor many of my pasta salads. It is possible to find low-sodium versions of soy sauce. "Light" soy sauce may refer to the color, but "lite" soy sauce is usually lower in sodium. Read the labels carefully.

Fish sauce is a mainstay of both Thai and Vietnamese cooking. A thin, salty brown sauce, it is made by salting small fish that are packed in wooden barrels. The liquid that runs off the fish is collected and bottled as fish sauce (or *nam pla* in Thailand and *nuoc mam* in Vietnam). The odor is more pungent than the flavor.

Oyster sauce is made from oysters, brine and soy sauce, cooked until it is richly flavored and thick. This dark brown sauce adds flavor without overpowering other ingredients.

Refrigerator Ingredients

EVERY SALAD calls for a unique combination of vegetables, meats or fish. But if you want to make pasta salads without prior planning, these are some ingredients you should keep on hand.

Buttermilk: Nonfat buttermilk makes a moist and creamy dressing. I use it extensively, rather than yogurt, which is thicker and tangier. Buttermilk has a shelf life of about 2 weeks and can be used in pancake batter or cornbread if it threatens to sour. If you prefer, you can substitute plain low-fat yogurt for buttermilk.

Lemons and Limes: I also stock lemons and limes in the refrigerator. Lemon juice, in particular, brightens the flavors of a salad.

Vegetables: I buy whatever looks good and then plan a salad around my choices. But I find it useful to have on hand scallions, red and green bell peppers, carrots, greens and, at least in the summer, tomatoes.

Cooking Tips

Pasta: Most packages of pasta provide cooking instructions. Bring a large pot of water (at least 4 quarts) to a boil. Add 1 tablespoon of salt. When the water comes to a rolling boil, add the pasta, stir occasionally, and follow the manufacturer's suggestions for timing the cooking. Regardless of the instructions, the pasta is done when it is firm and offers just a slight resistance when bitten. The Italian term is *al dente*, which translates "to the tooth."

Drain the pasta in a large colander, rinse gently under running water, then toss with oil, as the recipe directs. You can toss the pasta with the oil right in the colander. Very little, if any, oil will drip out—and you won't have to dirty an extra bowl.

Blanching Vegetables: Many of the recipes call for briefly blanching the vegetables, which sets the color and enhances the taste. To do this, boil enough water to cover the vegetables completely; usually 2 cups will do. Begin timing as soon as the vegetables are added to the water. Don't wait for the water to return to boiling, or the vegetables will be over-cooked. Remove from the heat as soon as the recipe specifies (10 to 45 seconds), drain the water, then plunge the vegetables into ice water to stop the cooking. When they are thoroughly cooled, drain well.

Chicken Preparations: Many of the chicken pasta salad recipes call for poached chicken. If you happen to have cooked chicken on hand, by all means substitute it. Figure about 2⅔ cups cooked chicken for each breast.

To poach chicken, place the meat in simmering liquid to cover—water, broth, white wine, or a combination. Add a handful of herbs or vegetables for extra flavor. Cook in the barely simmering water (do not boil) until the flesh is firm and white. Reserve the cooking liquid for soup stock.

It takes about 15 minutes to poach a chicken breast, roughly the same amount of time it takes to bring a big pot of water to a boil. However, if you have a microwave and want to save a little time, here is an alternative cooking method:

Place the breast halves side by side on a plate with the thicker areas pointing out. Cover with waxed paper. Microwave on high for 2 minutes. Rotate the plate a half turn, and microwave on high for 2 to 3 minutes. Test for doneness: the juices should run clear when the flesh is pierced with a fork. Remove the dish and cover with foil; allow the chicken to stand for 5 minutes before dicing and using.

Vegetable
Pasta Salads

Tomato-Mozzarella Pasta Salad

¾   pound farfalle, shells or cavatelli
3   tablespoons extra-virgin olive oil
2   pounds ripe tomatoes, cored and chopped
⅓   pound part-skim mozzarella, diced
½   cup chopped fresh basil
¼   cup chopped red onion
3   tablespoons red-wine vinegar
    Salt and freshly ground black pepper to taste
    Mixed salad greens, including sharp-tasting greens such as arugula or cress (optional)

1. Cook pasta in large pot of boiling salted water until just done. Drain and rinse thoroughly to cool. Place in large mixing bowl and toss with 1 tablespoon olive oil.

2. While pasta cooks, combine 2 tablespoons olive oil, tomatoes, mozzarella, basil, onion and vinegar in large mixing bowl. Season generously with salt and pepper. (Salad can be held for several hours by refrigerating pasta and greens in separate airtight containers. Tomato and cheese mixture can sit at room temperature for several hours.)

3. To serve, allow pasta to return to room temperature, if possible. Toss pasta with tomato and cheese mixture. Arrange bed of mixed salad greens on individual salad plates and heap pasta on top.

Makes 4 to 6 servings.

557 CALORIES PER SERVING: 22 G PROTEIN; 19 G FAT; 77 G CARBOHYDRATE; 195 MG SODIUM; 21 MG CHOLESTEROL.

Cheese Tortellini
With Red Pepper Dressing

While the water for the pasta boils, prepare the dressing and wash the spinach. The roasted red pepper dressing is delicious on green salads also.

SALAD

16–18	ounces fresh cheese tortellini
2	teaspoons extra-virgin olive oil
½	pound spinach or other greens, trimmed, washed and well dried

ROASTED RED PEPPER DRESSING

1	jar (7½ ounces) roasted red peppers, drained (about 3 peppers; to roast peppers, see page 13)
3	tablespoons sherry vinegar or balsamic vinegar
2	cloves garlic
1	tablespoon chopped fresh basil or 1 tablespoon chopped fresh parsley plus 1 teaspoon dried basil
2	teaspoons sugar
1	tablespoon extra-virgin olive oil
	Salt to taste

1. Prepare Salad: Cook tortellini in large pot of boiling salted water until just done. Drain and rinse thoroughly to cool. Place in large mixing bowl and toss with olive oil

2. Prepare Dressing: Combine red peppers, vinegar, garlic, basil and sugar in blender or food processor. Blend until smooth. Pour into bowl and whisk in olive oil. (Salad can be held for several hours, up to 1 day, by refrigerating tortellini and dressing in separate airtight containers. Wrap greens in moist paper toweling, place in plastic bag and refrigerate.)

3. Before serving, allow salad and dressing to return to room temperature, if possible. To serve, remix dressing and pour over tortellini and toss. Arrange spinach on platter or individual salad plates. Mound tortellini on top of spinach.

Makes 4 servings.

479 CALORIES PER SERVING: 16 G PROTEIN; 9 G FAT; 80 G CARBOHYDRATE; 103 MG SODIUM; 98 MG CHOLESTEROL.

Tortellini With Pesto

SALAD

16–18	ounces fresh cheese or meat tortellini
1	large carrot, trimmed, peeled and grated into long, thin shreds

PESTO DRESSING

1	cup fresh basil leaves
2	tablespoons grated sapsago cheese or Parmesan
2	cloves garlic
6	tablespoons defatted chicken broth
1	tablespoon extra-virgin olive oil

Salt and freshly ground black pepper to taste

1. Prepare Salad: Cook tortellini in large pot of boiling salted water until just done. Drain and rinse thoroughly to cool. Place in large mixing bowl. Add carrot and toss.

2. Prepare Dressing: Combine basil, cheese and garlic in food processor and process until well chopped. With motor running, drizzle in chicken broth and oil. (Salad can be held for several hours, up to 1 day, by refrigerating tortellini mixture and dressing in separate airtight containers.)

3. Before serving, let salad and pesto return to room temperature, if possible. To serve, remix dressing, pour over salad and toss gently. Add salt and pepper to taste.

Makes 4 servings.

453 CALORIES PER SERVING: 18 G PROTEIN; 8 G FAT; 78 G CARBOHYDRATE; 162 MG SODIUM; 100 MG CHOLESTEROL.

Creamy Pea and Pasta Salad

SALAD
½	pound shells or cavatelli
1	teaspoon extra-virgin olive oil
1½	pounds peas in pod, shelled (about 1½ cups)
1	large carrot, trimmed, peeled and diced
3	tablespoons chopped red onion

CREAMY LEMON-MINT DRESSING
½	cup buttermilk
½	cup chopped fresh mint leaves plus more for garnish
1	tablespoon extra-virgin olive oil
	Juice of 1 lemon
1	teaspoon grated lemon zest
½	teaspoon salt, or more to taste

1. Prepare Salad: Cook pasta in large pot of boiling salted water until just done. Drain and rinse thoroughly to cool. Place in large mixing bowl and toss with olive oil.

2. Blanch peas in boiling water to cover for 10 to 20 seconds. Plunge into ice water to stop cooking. Drain. Combine peas, carrot and red onion with pasta. Toss

3. Prepare Dressing: In blender, combine all ingredients. (Salad can be held for several hours, up to 1 day, by refrigerating pasta and dressing in separate airtight containers.)

4. Before serving, allow salad and dressing to return to room temperature, if possible. Pour dressing over salad and toss to mix. Add salt to taste, if needed. Spoon into serving bowl. Garnish with fresh mint leaves.

Makes 4 to 6 servings as a side dish.

340 CALORIES PER SERVING: 12 G PROTEIN; 6 G FAT; 58 G CARBOHYDRATE; 312 MG SODIUM; I MG CHOLESTEROL.

Here's a wonderful way to celebrate the season of fresh peas. If the peas come from your own garden, chances are you will have baby carrots, too, in which case they should be left whole and not diced.

Roasted Asparagus and Pasta Salad

Little preparation time is required for this simple, surprisingly rich salad, which is rather delicate in flavor and at its best when freshly made. Roasting rather than blanching the asparagus adds depth of flavor. It is important to use fresh herbs in the salad. Serve as a side dish.

1–1½   pounds asparagus, trimmed and cut diagonally into 1-inch pieces
1   red, yellow or purple bell pepper, cored, seeded and cut into 1-inch strips
3   tablespoons olive oil
Coarse salt
½   pound spirals or twists
Juice of 1 lemon
1–2   tablespoons chopped fresh herbs (basil, oregano or thyme)
Freshly ground black pepper to taste
¼   cup toasted pine nuts or sprigs of fresh herbs for garnish (optional)

1. Preheat oven to 500 degrees F and begin heating large pot of boiling salted water for pasta.

2. Combine asparagus and peppers in large mixing bowl. Toss with 2 tablespoons olive oil. Spread on baking sheet and sprinkle with coarse salt. Roast for about 7 minutes, until asparagus is tender when pierced with fork. Return to bowl. Stir to cool.

3. Cook pasta until just done. Drain and rinse thoroughly to cool. Toss with asparagus, along with remaining 1 tablespoon olive oil, lemon juice and fresh herbs. Season to taste with pepper and additional salt or herbs, if needed. Garnish with pine nuts or additional snipped fresh herbs. Serve at once.

Makes 4 to 6 servings as a side dish.

335 CALORIES PER SERVING: 9 G PROTEIN; 12 G FAT; 49 G CARBOHYDRATE; 475 MG SODIUM; 0 MG CHOLESTEROL.

Summer Vegetable Pasta Salad

My idea of a great summer meal: pasta with vegetables from the garden.

SALAD
¾	pound farfalle or small shells
1	can (2 ounces) anchovies packed in olive oil
½	pound green beans, trimmed and cut into 1½-inch lengths
1	small zucchini (about ½ pound), trimmed and chopped
2	large ripe tomatoes, cored and chopped
1	green bell pepper, cored, seeded and diced
1	small red onion, thinly sliced

BASIL DRESSING
1	cup fresh basil leaves, packed
	Juice of 1 lemon
	Juice of 1 orange
1	tablespoon red-wine vinegar
1	tablespoon olive oil (substitute oil from anchovies, if desired)

1. Prepare Salad: Cook pasta in large pot of boiling salted water until just done. Drain and rinse thoroughly to cool. Drain oil from anchovies, reserving 1 to 2 tablespoons. Place pasta in large mixing bowl and toss with 1 tablespoon anchovy oil.

2. Blanch green beans in boiling water for 15 seconds. Add zucchini and continue to blanch for 15 seconds. Drain; plunge vegetables in ice water to stop cooking. Drain again.

3. Chop anchovies into quarters. Combine anchovies, green beans, zucchini, tomatoes, green pepper and half the onions with pasta and toss.

4. Prepare Dressing: Combine basil, lemon juice, orange juice and vinegar in blender. Pour into small bowl and whisk in olive or anchovy oil. (Salad can be held for up to 12 hours by refrigerating pasta and dressing in separate airtight containers.)

5. Before serving, allow salad and dressing to return to room temperature, if possible. Remix dressing and pour over salad; toss well. Spoon into serving bowl or onto individual plates; garnish with remaining onion.

Makes 4 to 6 servings.

453 CALORIES PER SERVING: 18 G PROTEIN; 7 G FAT; 81 G CARBOHYDRATE; 539 MG SODIUM; 12 MG CHOLESTEROL.

Tex-Mex Pasta Salad

¾	pound wagon wheels
2	teaspoons extra-virgin olive oil
1	pound peeled and cooked small shrimp (optional)
2	cloves garlic, finely chopped
½	cup chopped fresh cilantro
4	ripe tomatoes, cored and chopped
2	scallions, trimmed and chopped
1	green bell pepper, cored, seeded and chopped
2–3	hot peppers, seeded and chopped
1	cup corn kernels, fresh or frozen
2	avocados, diced
½–¾	cup V8 or tomato juice
	Salt and freshly ground black pepper to taste
	Chopped hot peppers or few sprigs of cilantro for garnish

1. Cook pasta in large pot of boiling salted water until just done. Drain and rinse thoroughly to cool. Place in large mixing bowl and toss with olive oil.

2. In another large mixing bowl, combine shrimp, if using, garlic, cilantro and vegetables, except avocado. Toss well. Add to pasta and toss. (To prepare in advance, combine all ingredients, except avocados and V8 or tomato juice, and refrigerate, covered.)

3. Just before serving, add avocados to salad and toss gently. Add V8 or tomato juice and salt and pepper to taste. Toss gently to avoid breaking pasta.

4. To serve, transfer to serving bowl and garnish with hot peppers or cilantro.

Makes 4 to 6 servings.

580 CALORIES PER SERVING: 16 G PROTEIN; 19 G FAT; 90 G CARBOHYDRATE; 130 MG SODIUM; 0 MG CHOLESTEROL.

Black Bean Pasta Salad

SALAD
¾ pound radiatore or other medium-size pasta
1 tablespoon olive oil
1 can (15 ounces) black beans, rinsed and drained (about 1½ cups dried beans, cooked)
1 red bell pepper, cored, seeded and diced
1 green bell pepper, cored, seeded and diced
1 cup diced jicama, peeled
½ cup diced red onion

DRESSING
¾ cup chopped fresh cilantro
½ cup defatted chicken broth
3 tablespoons orange juice
3 tablespoons red-wine vinegar
1 teaspoon ground cumin
½ teaspoon chili powder, or more to taste
1 tablespoon olive oil

Salt to taste
Chopped jalapeño pepper for garnish (optional)

1. Prepare Salad: Cook pasta in large pot of boiling salted water until just done. Drain and rinse thoroughly to cool. Place in large mixing bowl and toss with olive oil. Add beans and vegetables to pasta.

2. Prepare Dressing: Combine cilantro, chicken broth, orange juice, vinegar, cumin and chili powder in a blender. Pour into small bowl and whisk in olive oil. (Salad can be held for several hours, up to 1 day, by refrigerating pasta and dressing in separate airtight containers.)

3. Before serving, allow salad and dressing to return to room temperature, if possible. Remix dressing and pour over salad; toss gently. Add salt and chili powder to taste; garnish with chopped hot pepper, if using.

Makes 4 to 6 servings.

519 CALORIES PER SERVING: 19 G PROTEIN; 9 G FAT; 91 G CARBOHYDRATE; 108 MG SODIUM; 0 MG CHOLESTEROL.

The flavors of the Southwest—black beans, cilantro and crunchy, sweet jicama—inspired this exotic salad. Salsa passed at the table will add another layer of flavor. If you haven't already tried jicama—that brown-skinned root vegetable you have seen in the produce department—now is your chance. Jicama's sweet nutty flesh is good raw or cooked. Peel it just before using and enjoy its crisp texture.

Three-Bean Pasta Salad

SALAD

¾	pound tricolor twists
1	tablespoon extra-virgin olive oil
½	pound green beans, trimmed, cut into 1½-inch lengths
½	pound wax beans, trimmed, cut into 1½-inch lengths
1	can (15 ounces) dark red kidney beans, drained and rinsed
¼	cup minced red onion
2	stalks celery, finely chopped
1	carrot, trimmed, peeled and finely chopped

SPICY TOMATO DRESSING

1½	cups V8 juice
2	tablespoons red-wine vinegar
2	cloves garlic
1	teaspoon sugar
½	teaspoon chili powder, or more to taste
1	tablespoon extra-virgin olive oil

Salt and freshly ground black pepper to taste

1. Prepare Salad: Cook pasta in large pot of boiling salted water until just done. Drain and rinse thoroughly to cool. Place in large mixing bowl and toss with olive oil.

2. Blanch green beans and wax beans in boiling water to cover for 30 seconds. Drain, plunge into ice water to stop cooking and drain again. Combine green beans, wax beans and kidney beans, onion, celery and carrot with pasta. Toss well.

3. Prepare Dressing: Combine V8 juice, vinegar, garlic, sugar and chili powder in a blender. Pour into small bowl and whisk in oil. (Salad can be held for several hours, up to 1 day, by refrigerating pasta in air-tight container. Dressing can be held at room temperature.)

4. Just before serving, pour dressing over salad. Season with salt and pepper and transfer to serving bowl.

Makes 6 to 10 servings as a side dish.

348 CALORIES PER SERVING: 13 G PROTEIN; 5 G FAT; 63 G CARBOHYDRATE; 450 MG SODIUM; 0 MG CHOLESTEROL.

Summer Eggplant Pasta Salad

1   pound shells, cavatelli or twists
3   tablespoons olive oil
1–1½   pounds eggplant (1 medium-size eggplant), peeled and sliced
          lengthwise, about ⅜ inch thick
2   cans (5.5 ounces each) V8 juice, or more to taste
½   pound zucchini (1 small), trimmed, quartered and sliced
1½   tablespoons red-wine vinegar
1   red bell pepper, cored, seeded and diced
2   cloves garlic, finely chopped
1   tablespoon capers, drained
¼   cup chopped fresh parsley
2   tablespoons chopped fresh oregano or 2 teaspoons dried
          Salt and freshly ground black pepper to taste

1. Cook pasta in large pot of boiling salted water until just done. While pasta cooks, preheat broiler. Drain pasta and rinse thoroughly to cool. Place in large mixing bowl and toss with 1 tablespoon olive oil.

2. Brush 1 tablespoon oil on baking sheet. Arrange eggplant on baking sheet and brush with remaining 1 tablespoon oil. Broil for about 15 minutes, turning occasionally and basting with V8 juice as needed to keep eggplant moist. When eggplant is tender and juicy, remove from broiler. Dice.

3. Blanch zucchini in boiling water to cover for about 45 seconds. Rinse, plunge into cold water to stop cooking; drain well. Combine pasta, eggplant, zucchini, remaining V8 juice and remaining ingredients. Toss well to mix. Taste and add salt and freshly ground black pepper.

4. Serve at room temperature. If you are not serving immediately, hold in refrigerator in tightly covered container, but bring to room temperature before serving. Moisten with additional V8 juice if needed.

Makes 4 to 6 servings.

582 CALORIES PER SERVING: 16 G PROTEIN; 13 G FAT; 100 G CARBOHYDRATE; 335 MG SODIUM; 0 MG CHOLESTEROL.

This hearty vegetarian salad takes its inspiration from the intensely flavorful mélange of eggplant, tomatoes, onions, celery and olives known as caponata, which is popular in Sicily as an antipasto. Here, the olives are replaced by a few tablespoons of olive oil, and nonfat V-8 juice makes a surprisingly flavorful dressing. This salad can form the basis of a wonderful summer meal, accompanied by a green salad and fresh corn on the cob. Or serve it as a side dish with a simply prepared grilled cutlet.

Lemon-Roasted Zucchini Pasta Salad

¾   pound twists or other medium-size pasta
2   teaspoons extra-virgin olive oil

LEMON-THYME DRESSING
    Juice of 2 lemons
    Zest of 1 lemon
¼   cup chopped fresh lemon thyme or regular thyme
2   shallots, coarsely chopped
2   tablespoons extra virgin olive oil

½   cup dry-pack sun-dried tomatoes
    Vegetable-oil cooking spray
3   medium-size zucchini (about 1½ pounds), quartered
        lengthwise, then sliced
½   red bell pepper, cored, seeded and cut into thin strips
¼   pound feta cheese
    Salt and freshly ground black pepper
    Sprigs of lemon thyme (optional)

1. Cook pasta in large pot of boiling salted water until just done. Drain and rinse thoroughly to cool. Place in large mixing bowl and toss with 2 teaspoons olive oil. Set aside. Preheat oven to 500 degrees F.

2. Prepare Dressing: Combine lemon juice, zest, thyme and shallots in a blender and process until well blended. Pour into small bowl and whisk in oil.

3. Soften sun-dried tomatoes in boiling water to cover for about 10 minutes. Drain well and cut into small pieces.

4. Spray baking sheet with vegetable-oil cooking spray. Place zucchini in another large mixing bowl. Add half the dressing and toss to coat well. Pour onto baking sheet and spread out to single layer. Roast for 5 minutes, then return zucchini to mixing bowl. Stir gently to cool.

(continued on page 36)

5. Combine zucchini, red pepper, sun-dried tomatoes and remaining dressing with pasta. Toss well. Crumble feta cheese. Set aside 1 tablespoon for garnish and mix in remainder. Season to taste with salt and pepper.

6. To serve, spoon into salad bowl and garnish with reserved feta cheese and sprigs of lemon thyme.

Makes 4 to 6 servings.

557 CALORIES PER SERVING: 19 G PROTEIN; 17 G FAT; 85 G CARBOHYDRATE; 342 MG SODIUM; 25 MG CHOLESTEROL.

Feta Pasta Salad

This unusually hearty vegetarian salad pairs perfectly with a rustic, whole-grain loaf of bread to make a satisfying summer meal.

¾   pound wagon wheels, twists, shells or cavatelli
3   tablespoons extra-virgin olive oil
1   medium-size zucchini (1–1½ pounds), trimmed, quartered and
      sliced
1   green bell pepper, cored, seeded and diced
1   onion, halved and sliced
1   tomato, cored and coarsely chopped plus 1 tomato, cored and
      cut in wedges for garnish
⅔   cup coarsely chopped fresh parsley
¼   pound feta cheese
1   teaspoon dried oregano or 1 tablespoon chopped fresh
      Juice of 2 lemons
6   cups sharp-tasting greens (cress, arugula)

1. Cook pasta in large pot of boiling salted water until just done. Drain and rinse thoroughly to cool. Place in large mixing bowl and toss with 1 tablespoon olive oil.

2. Blanch zucchini in boiling water to cover for 30 seconds. Plunge into ice water to stop cooking, then drain.

3. In another large mixing bowl, combine zucchini, pepper, onion, chopped tomato, parsley, feta cheese and oregano. Toss to mix. Add lemon juice and remaining 2 tablespoons olive oil and toss again. (Salad can be held for several hours by refrigerating pasta and vegetables in separate airtight containers.)

4. Before serving, allow salad and dressing to return to room temperature, if possible. Combine pasta with vegetables and toss well. To serve, place bed or ring of greens on large serving platter or on individual serving plates, mound salad in center and garnish with tomato wedges.

Makes 4 to 6 servings.

568 CALORIES PER SERVING: 19 G PROTEIN; 19 G FAT; 83 G CARBOHYDRATE; 340 MG SODIUM; 25 MG CHOLESTEROL.

Four-Pepper Pasta Salad

SALAD
¾	pound penne or other medium-size pasta
1	tablespoon extra-virgin olive oil
1	yellow bell pepper, cored, seeded and thinly sliced
1	green bell pepper, cored, seeded and thinly sliced
1	purple pepper, cored, seeded and thinly sliced
3	ounces Monterey Jack or other mild semi-soft cheese, thinly sliced
1	small onion, sliced in rings
1½	tablespoons capers, drained
½	cup chopped fresh parsley

RED PEPPER VINAIGRETTE
1	jar (7½ ounces) roasted red peppers, drained (about 3 roasted peppers; to roast peppers, see page 13)
3	tablespoons balsamic vinegar
1	tablespoon extra-virgin olive oil

Salt and freshly ground black pepper to taste

1. Prepare Salad: Cook pasta in large pot of boiling salted water until just done. Drain and rinse thoroughly to cool. Place in large mixing bowl and toss with olive oil.

2. Cut peppers and cheese into lengths to match pasta, about 2½ inches. Combine peppers, cheese, onion, capers and parsley with pasta.

3. Prepare Dressing: Combine roasted peppers, vinegar and olive oil in blender and process until smooth. (Salad can be held for several hours by refrigerating pasta and dressing in separate airtight containers.)

4. Before serving, allow salad and dressing to return to room temperature, if possible. Pour dressing over salad and toss well. Add salt and pepper to taste. This salad will hold up well for 1 day. Refresh leftovers with a little balsamic vinegar or lemon juice.

Makes 4 to 6 servings.

519 CALORIES PER SERVING: 18 G PROTEIN; 15 G FAT; 78 G CARBOHYDRATE; 190 MG SODIUM; 19 MG CHOLESTEROL.

The dressing is made from a base of pureed roasted red peppers, while the salad contains yellow, green and purple peppers. Capers are essential for bringing out the flavor. This colorful salad makes a nice side dish, especially good for taking on a picnic: There's nothing to spoil in the heat, and the ingredients will hold up to a little jostling.

Pesto Pasta Salad

SALAD
¾	pound linguine
1	tablespoon extra-virgin olive oil
1	pound asparagus, trimmed and cut into 2-to-3-inch lengths
½	pound sugar snap peas, trimmed
½	red or yellow bell pepper, cored, seeded and sliced into 2-to-3-inch lengths
	Salt to taste

PESTO DRESSING
2	cups fresh basil leaves
3	tablespoons grated sapsago cheese or Parmesan
3	cloves garlic
2	tablespoons extra-virgin olive oil
½	cup defatted chicken broth
2	tablespoons red-wine vinegar

1. Prepare Salad: Cook pasta in large pot of boiling salted water until just done. Drain and rinse thoroughly to cool. Place in large mixing bowl and toss with olive oil.

2. Blanch asparagus in boiling water to cover for 45 seconds. Drain; plunge into ice water to stop cooking. Combine asparagus, sugar snap peas and bell pepper with pasta. Toss gently.

3. Prepare Dressing: In food processor, combine basil, cheese and garlic. Process until finely chopped. With motor running, drizzle in oil, then chicken broth and vinegar. (Salad can be held for several hours, up to 1 day, by refrigerating pasta and dressing in separate airtight containers.)

4. Before serving, allow salad and dressing to return to room temperature, if possible. To serve, remix dressing, pour over salad and toss gently.

Makes 4 to 6 servings.

507 CALORIES PER SERVING: 18 G PROTEIN; 14 G FAT; 79 G CARBOHYDRATE; 123 MG SODIUM; 4 MG CHOLESTEROL.

Any combination of vegetables will work with pesto dressing, but one of my favorites is a mixture of asparagus, sugar snap peas and sweet peppers. Try to cut all the vegetables to the same length—in this case, keep them similar in size to the snap peas. If the asparagus spears are particularly broad, slice them in halves or quarters.

Broccoli Pasta Salad With Lemon-Tahini Dressing

SALAD
- ½ pound farfalle or twists
- 1 teaspoon sesame oil
- 1 pound broccoli (1 large or 2 small stalks), stems peeled, florets separated
- 1 red bell pepper, cored, seeded and cut into thin strips
- ¼ red onion, thinly sliced

LEMON-TAHINI DRESSING
- 1 cup chopped fresh parsley, packed
- ½ cup white grape juice
- Juice of 2 lemons
- 3 cloves garlic
- 2 tablespoons tahini

- Salt and freshly ground black pepper to taste
- 1 tablespoon sesame seeds, toasted (optional)

1. Prepare Salad: Cook pasta in large pot of boiling salted water until just done. Drain and rinse thoroughly to cool. Place in large mixing bowl and toss with sesame oil.

2. Cut broccoli stems into thin strips. Cut florets into small pieces. Blanch broccoli in boiling water to cover for about 30 seconds. Plunge into ice water to stop cooking. Drain. Combine broccoli, red pepper and red onion slices with pasta.

3. Prepare Dressing: Combine all ingredients in blender. (Salad can be held for several hours, up to 1 day, by refrigerating pasta and dressing in separate airtight containers.)

(continued on page 44)

4. Before serving, allow salad and dressing to return to room temperature, if possible. Remix dressing. Pour over salad and toss well; taste and add salt and pepper. Serve from large bowl, garnished with toasted sesame seeds, if using.

Makes 4 to 6 servings as a side dish.

340 CALORIES PER SERVING: 12 G PROTEIN; 7 G FAT; 61 G CARBOHYDRATE; 42 MG SODIUM; 0 MG CHOLESTEROL.

Winter Pasta Salad

SALAD
¾	pound tricolor pasta twists
2	teaspoons extra-virgin olive oil
1	stalk broccoli
½	head cauliflower
½	cup dry-pack sun-dried tomatoes
½	cup roasted red pepper, cut into thin strips (to roast peppers, see page 13, or used bottled)

DRESSING
1	cup defatted chicken broth
¼	cup red-wine vinegar
2	cloves garlic, finely chopped
1	teaspoon Dijon-style mustard
1	teaspoon dried oregano
1	tablespoon extra-virgin olive oil

Salt and freshly ground black pepper to taste

1. Prepare Salad: Cook pasta in large pot of boiling salted water until just done. Drain and rinse thoroughly to cool. Place in large mixing bowl and toss with olive oil.

2. Chop broccoli and cauliflower so the pieces are bite-size or smaller. You should have 5 to 6 cups. Blanch in boiling water to cover for 45 seconds to tenderize slightly and set color. Plunge into ice water to stop cooking; drain. Soften sun-dried tomatoes in boiling water to cover for about 10 minutes. Drain.

3. Combine broccoli, cauliflower, tomatoes and red pepper with pasta. Toss.

4. Prepare Dressing: Combine chicken broth, vinegar, garlic, mustard and oregano in blender. Pour into small bowl and whisk in olive oil. (Salad can be held for several hours, up to 1 day, by refrigerating pasta and dressing in separate airtight containers.)

Sun-dried tomatoes and roasted peppers provide an echo of summer in this recipe. Be sure to select dry-pack tomatoes, not the oil-packed variety.

(continued on page 46)

5. Before serving, allow salad and dressing to return to room temperature, if possible. Remix dressing, pour over salad and toss. Add salt and pepper to taste.

Makes 4 to 6 servings.

426 CALORIES PER SERVING: 16 G PROTEIN; 7 G FAT; 79 G CARBOHYDRATE; 262 MG SODIUM; 0 MG CHOLESTEROL.

Cold Sesame Noodles

I've experimented with this recipe over the years (including once in five-gallon buckets for my sister's wedding), until I've gotten it just right: light, moist and spicy, but not overpoweringly hot. The salad may seem a bit soupy when first made, but don't worry, the noodles will rapidly absorb the excess liquid. Because it is so moist, this dish holds up unusually well on a buffet table. Tahini, or ground sesame seed paste, is available in most larger supermarkets. Chili paste with garlic, which is readily found wherever Asian foods are sold, contributes heat to the dish. If you are unsure how much spiciness you will enjoy, start with just ½ teaspoon. Then after the salad is mixed, you can add more. And, of course, if you love spicy foods . . .

NOODLES

¾ pound linguine or 1 pound fresh Chinese noodles
1 tablespoon sesame oil
¼ pound snow peas, trimmed
3 scallions, trimmed, slivered and cut into 3-inch lengths

SPICY SESAME DRESSING

1 cup defatted chicken broth
¼ cup tahini
1 tablespoon Chinese rice wine
1½ teaspoons chili paste with garlic, or more to taste
1 teaspoon reduced-sodium soy sauce

1 carrot, trimmed, peeled and cut into thin strips for garnish

1. Prepare Salad: Cook noodles in large pot of boiling salted water until just done. Drain and rinse thoroughly to cool. Place in large mixing bowl and toss with sesame oil.

2. Blanch snow peas in boiling water to cover for just 10 seconds. Plunge into cold water to stop cooking. Drain. Combine snow peas and scallions with noodles.

3. Prepare Dressing: In blender, combine all dressing ingredients. Pour over salad and toss well. (Salad can be served immediately or held for several hours, covered, in refrigerator. For longer storage, refrigerate pasta and dressing in separate airtight containers for up to 1 day. Bring to room temperature before serving.)

4. To serve, garnish with carrot.

Makes 4 to 6 servings as an appetizer.

490 CALORIES PER SERVING: 16 G PROTEIN; 14 G FAT; 76 G CARBOHYDRATE; 292 MG SODIUM; 0 MG CHOLESTEROL.

Cold Japanese-Style Noodles

SALAD

12	ounces soba (Japanese buckwheat noodles)
1	daikon (Oriental radish), peeled and grated into thin shreds
1	carrot, peeled and grated into thin shreds
1	cucumber, peeled, seeded and cut into thin strips
3	scallions, trimmed and chopped
2	tablespoons rice-wine vinegar
1	tablespoon mirin or sweet sherry
1	teaspoon sugar
½	teaspoon salt

JAPANESE DRESSING

1¼	cups defatted chicken stock
6	tablespoons reduced-sodium soy sauce
6	tablespoons mirin
2	teaspoons peeled, grated fresh ginger
2	scallions, trimmed and finely chopped
1	tablespoon sesame seeds, toasted, for garnish

1. Prepare Salad: Cook soba in large pot of boiling salted water until just done, about 5 minutes. Drain and rinse thoroughly to cool.

2. Combine vegetables in bowl. Add vinegar, mirin, sugar and salt. Mix well.

3. Prepare Dressing: Combine all ingredients and mix well. (Salad can be held for up to 12 hours by refrigerating noodles, vegetables and dressing in separate airtight containers.)

4. To serve, arrange noodles on large platter. Arrange vegetables on top. Garnish with sesame seeds. Pass dressing at table.

Makes 4 to 6 servings.

373 CALORIES PER SERVING: 17 G PROTEIN; 3 G FAT; 73 G CARBOHYDRATE; 1942 MG SODIUM; 0 MG CHOLESTEROL.

This salad offers a marvelous balance of flavors and textures—chewy soba noodles, crisp vegetables and a dressing that is sweet, salty and sour all at the same time. The amount of dressing may seem excessive, but don't be surprised if your guests drink up the extra in their bowls once the noodles have been devoured. If you have the time, make the salad early in the day and serve it icy cold. Since the dressing is quite thin, serve the salad in bowls rather than on plates. A more authentically Japanese recipe would require dashi, a stock make from dried bonito shavings and kombu, a type of kelp, in the dressing. But for convenience, chicken stock is used here. Mirin is a sweet Japanese rice wine.

Seafood and Fish
Pasta Salads

Vietnamese Shrimp Salad With Rice Vermicelli

1	pound rice vermicelli
⅔	cup fish sauce
½	cup white vinegar
⅓	cup sugar
2	cloves garlic, finely chopped
1	pound medium shrimp, peeled and deveined
½	lemon
1	carrot, trimmed, peeled and cut into thin strips
1	cucumber, peeled, seeded and cut into thin strips
1	scallion, including green parts, trimmed and chopped
2–3	tablespoons chopped fresh cilantro for garnish
2–3	tablespoons chopped roasted peanuts for garnish

1. Cook rice vermicelli in large pot of boiling water for about 5 minutes, until tender but still firm. Drain and rinse thoroughly to cool.

2. Combine fish sauce, vinegar, sugar and garlic in small saucepan. Heat gently, stirring constantly, until sugar is dissolved. Set aside to cool.

3. Add shrimp and lemon half to medium-size pot of boiling water and poach shrimp in barely simmering water until pink and firm, about 2 to 3 minutes. Drain, discard lemon and set aside.

4. Place rice vermicelli in large mixing bowl and pour half of the dressing over. Toss well. Add shrimp, carrot, cucumber and scallions; toss again.

5. Serve immediately or hold for up to 1 day by refrigerating in airtight container. To serve, place on individual salad plates and garnish each with sprinkling of cilantro and peanuts. Pass remaining dressing at table.

Makes 4 servings as a main course or 6 as an appetizer.

626 CALORIES PER SERVING: 27 G PROTEIN; 5 G FAT; 116 G CARBOHYDRATE; 520 MG SODIUM; 130 MG CHOLESTEROL.

With no oil in the dressing, this light salad makes a delicious starter for an adventurous meal, but I also enjoy it by itself. One of the best salads for making ahead, it holds up well in the refrigerator (be sure it is well covered). To save time, you can purchase already cooked and peeled shrimp. The rice vermicelli and fish sauce (nuoc mam or nam pla) are available wherever Asian foods are sold.
(See photograph on the front cover.)

This ethereally light and beautiful salad was inspired by the flavors of Vietnamese cooking. The combination of citrus and mint makes it a delightfully cooling meal. You can save time by purchasing cooked and peeled shrimp.

Shrimp and Rice Noodle Salad With Minted Grapefruit

1	pound rice noodles or rice sticks
¾	pound medium shrimp, peeled and deveined
1	1-inch cube fresh ginger
6	tablespoons fish sauce
	Juice of 1 orange
	Juice of 1 lemon
2	teaspoons canola or peanut oil
1	red bell pepper, cored, seeded and cut into thin strips
2	seedless grapefruits, peeled and sectioned
4	thin slices red onion, halved
½	cup fresh mint leaves, chopped
	Additional mint leaves for garnish

1. Cook rice noodles in large pot of boiling water for about 5 minutes, until tender but still firm. Drain and rinse thoroughly to cool. Place in large bowl.

2. Add shrimp and ginger to medium-size pot of boiling water and poach shrimp until pink and firm, about 3 minutes. Drain, discard ginger and set shrimp aside.

3. Combine fish sauce, orange juice and lemon juice. Whisk in oil. Pour dressing over rice noodles. Toss well. Add shrimp, red pepper, grapefruit, red onion and mint. Toss again. Garnish with mint leaves. Serve immediately or hold for up to 1 day by refrigerating in airtight container. Refresh with a few squirts of fish sauce before serving.

Makes 4 to 6 servings.

537 CALORIES PER SERVING: 13 G PROTEIN; 4 G FAT; 113 G CARBOHYDRATE; 341 MG SODIUM; 97 MG CHOLESTEROL.

Medium shrimp (41 to 60 per pound) are best for this salad. Cooking them yourself in a ginger- and garlic-scented liquid adds flavor, but to save time, you can buy cooked shrimp of any size.

Chinese Sesame Shrimp and Noodle Salad

SALAD

1	pound fresh Chinese noodles or ¾ pound linguine
1	tablespoon sesame oil
2	cloves garlic, slivered
1	2-inch piece fresh ginger, sliced
1	pound medium shrimp, peeled and deveined
1	large stalk broccoli, stem peeled
½	red bell pepper, cored, seeded and cut into thin strips
4	scallions, trimmed, slivered and cut into 2-inch lengths

SWEET SOY DRESSING

2	tablespoons rice-wine vinegar
1	tablespoon sherry or Chinese rice wine
4	teaspoons reduced-sodium soy sauce
1	teaspoon hoisin sauce
2	cloves garlic, crushed through a press
1	teaspoon peeled, grated fresh ginger
2	tablespoons sesame oil
2	tablespoons sesame seeds, toasted

1. Prepare Salad: Cook noodles in large pot of boiling salted water until just done. Drain and rinse thoroughly to cool. Place in large mixing bowl and toss with sesame oil.

2. Fill medium-size saucepan with water, add slivered garlic and ginger. Bring to boil. Add shrimp and poach in barely simmering water for about 3 minutes, until pink and firm. Drain and rinse in cool water. Set aside in another bowl.

3. Cut broccoli stem into thin strips and separate top of broccoli into small florets. Blanch stems in boiling water to cover for about 30 seconds. Plunge into ice water to stop cooking and drain.

(continued on page 56)

4. Add broccoli stems, red pepper and scallions to noodles and toss well to distribute vegetables evenly.

5. Blanch broccoli florets in boiling water to cover for about 20 seconds. Plunge into ice water to stop cooking. Drain and add to shrimp.

6. Prepare Dressing: Combine all ingredients, except sesame oil, in small bowl. Whisk in sesame oil. (Salad can be held for several hours by refrigerating shrimp and broccoli florets, noodles and remaining ingredients, and dressing, in three separate airtight containers.)

6. Before serving, allow noodles and dressing to return to room temperature, if possible. Remix dressing and pour over noodles and vegetables. To serve, arrange on platter, scattering broccoli florets and shrimp over noodles. Sprinkle sesame seeds over all.

Makes 4 to 6 servings.

593 CALORIES PER SERVING: 32 G PROTEIN; 16 G FAT; 79 G CARBOHYDRATE; 422 MG SODIUM; 220 MG CHOLESTEROL.

Neptune's Delight

This is a salad of indulgence, with shrimp and crabmeat lightly seasoned with cilantro and lime.

SALAD

¾	pound shells or other medium-size pasta
1	tablespoon extra-virgin olive oil
1	pound medium or large shrimp, peeled and deveined
½	lemon
½	pound lump crabmeat, picked over
½	cup frozen peas
1	red bell pepper, cored, seeded and diced
3	scallions, trimmed and chopped

CILANTRO DRESSING

½	cup defatted chicken broth
½	cup chopped fresh cilantro
½	cup chopped fresh parsley
	Juice of 1½ lemons
	Juice of 1 lime
2	tablespoons red-wine vinegar
1	tablespoon extra-virgin olive oil
	Salt and freshly ground black pepper to taste

1. Prepare Salad: Cook pasta in large pot of boiling salted water until just done. Drain and rinse thoroughly to cool. Place in large mixing bowl and toss with olive oil.

2. Add shrimp and lemon to pot of boiling water and poach shrimp in barely simmering water until pink and firm, about 3 minutes. Drain, discard lemon, and plunge shrimp into ice water to stop cooking; drain again. Combine shrimp, crabmeat and vegetables with pasta. Toss gently.

3. Prepare Dressing: Combine ingredients, except oil, in blender. Pour into small bowl and whisk in oil. (Salad may be held for several hours by refrigerating pasta and dressing in separate airtight containers.)

4. Just before serving, remix dressing and pour over salad. Toss gently. Add salt and pepper to taste. Spoon into serving bowl.

Makes 4 to 6 servings.

536 CALORIES PER SERVING: 36 G PROTEIN; 10 G FAT; 74 G CARBOHYDRATE; 411 MG SODIUM; 155 MG CHOLESTEROL.

Orzo Shrimp Salad

SALAD

1	pound orzo
2	teaspoons extra-virgin olive oil
1	pound peeled, cooked small shrimp
1	cup frozen peas
¼	cup chopped fresh basil
3	ounces feta cheese, crumbled

TOMATO DRESSING

4	medium-size ripe tomatoes (1 pound), cored and chopped
2	tablespoons extra-virgin olive oil
1	tablespoon red-wine vinegar
1	teaspoon fresh lemon juice
	Salt and freshly ground black pepper to taste
	Salad greens and additional basil (optional)

1. Prepare Salad: Cook orzo in large pot of boiling salted water until just done. Drain and rinse thoroughly to cool. Place in large mixing bowl and toss with olive oil. Add remaining salad ingredients and toss.

2. Prepare Dressing: Combine all ingredients in bowl and mix well. Add dressing to salad and toss well. (Salad will hold for several hours in refrigerator, but add basil and feta cheese at last minute.)

3. Before serving, allow salad to return to room temperature. Serve in large bowl or on individual plates lined with salad greens. Garnish with additional basil.

Makes 4 to 6 servings.

748 CALORIES PER SERVING: 45 G PROTEIN; 18 G FAT; 101 G CARBOHYDRATE; 507 MG SODIUM; 240 MG CHOLESTEROL.

A dish so quick to prepare, you'll be able to make a green salad to go with it while you wait for the pasta water to boil.

Crab and Cress Pasta Salad

¾   pound penne or ziti
3   tablespoons extra-virgin olive oil
¾   pound lump crabmeat, picked over
3   tablespoons minced fresh chives or scallions
2   tablespoons capers, drained
     Juice of 2 lemons or more to taste
2   bunches watercress (about 8 ounces), large stems discarded, chopped in half
2   ripe tomatoes, cored and cut in wedges, for garnish
     Salt and freshly ground pepper to taste

1. Cook pasta in large pot of boiling salted water until just done. Drain and rinse thoroughly to cool. Place in large mixing bowl and toss with 1 tablespoon olive oil.

2. In another bowl, combine crabmeat, chives or scallions, capers, remaining 2 tablespoons olive oil and lemon juice. Toss gently. Add to pasta and toss again. Add salt and pepper to taste and more lemon juice if needed.

3. Arrange watercress around outside edge of large serving platter. Mound pasta mixture in middle. Garnish with tomatoes and serve at once.

Makes 4 servings.

520 CALORIES PER SERVING: 28 G PROTEIN; 13 G FAT; 72 G CARBOHYDRATE; 370 MG SODIUM; 50 MG CHOLESTEROL.

Grilled Tuna Pasta Salad

TUNA
- ¾   pound tuna steak
-     Juice of 1 lemon
- 1   tablespoon extra-virgin olive oil
- 1   clove garlic, finely chopped
- ½   teaspoon dried rosemary

SALAD
- ¾   pound penne or ziti
- 1   tablespoon extra-virgin olive oil
- ¼   pound green beans, trimmed and cut into 2-inch lengths
- ½   red bell pepper, cored, seeded and cut into thin strips
- 1   ripe tomato, cored and chopped
- 3   tablespoons chopped chives or scallions

CAPER DRESSING
- 3   tablespoons defatted chicken broth
- 3   tablespoons red-wine vinegar
-     Juice of 1 lemon
- 1   clove garlic, finely chopped
- 1   teaspoon capers, drained
- 1   teaspoon olive oil

-     Salt and freshly ground black pepper to taste
- 10   ounces fresh spinach, washed, trimmed and torn into bite-size pieces (approximately 7 cups)
- 5   brine-cured black olives (optional)

1. Prepare Tuna: In a shallow bowl large enough to hold tuna, mix lemon juice, olive oil, garlic and rosemary and marinate tuna while you preheat grill. Heat large pot of salted water for pasta.

2. Grill tuna for about 5 minutes per side, until firm and opaque throughout. Cut into bite-size pieces.

3. Prepare Salad: Cook pasta until just done. Drain and rinse thoroughly to cool. Place in large mixing bowl and toss with olive oil. Blanch

(continued on page 62)

Canned tuna can't hold a candle to fresh tuna that has been marinated in a rosemary-garlic marinade, then grilled. Add a loaf of French bread and a bottle of crisp white wine, and dinner is complete.

green beans in boiling water for 30 seconds. Plunge into ice water to stop cooking; drain. Combine tuna, green beans, red pepper, tomato and chives or scallions with pasta.

4. Prepare Dressing: Combine chicken broth, vinegar, lemon juice, garlic and capers in small bowl. Whisk in olive oil. (Salad can be held for several hours by refrigerating pasta and dressing in separate airtight containers. Wrap spinach in moist paper toweling, place in plastic bag and refrigerate.)

5. Before serving, allow salad and dressing to return to room temperature, if possible. Remix dressing and pour over salad; toss well. Add salt and generous amount of pepper to taste. To serve, arrange bed of spinach in large serving bowl or on individual salad plates. Top with salad. Garnish with chopped black olives, if using.

Makes 4 to 6 servings.

574 CALORIES PER SERVING: 36 G PROTEIN; 14 G FAT; 75 G CARBOHYDRATE; 150 MG SODIUM; 35 MG CHOLESTEROL.

Tuna Macaroni Salad

This version may be a little crunchier and more flavorful than Mom's picnic standard. It is also lower in fat than Mom's.

¾   pound elbow macaroni
2   large stalks celery
1   large carrot, trimmed and peeled
½   onion
1   cup fresh parsley
1   can (about 6 ounces) water-packed tuna, drained
¾   cup fat-free mayonnaise
1   tablespoon extra-virgin olive oil
    Juice of 2 lemons
2   tablespoons pickle relish (optional)
    Salt and freshly ground black pepper to taste

1. Cook pasta in large pot of boiling salted water until just done. Drain and rinse thoroughly to cool. Place in large mixing bowl.

2. Using food processor fitted with steel blade, finely chop vegetables and parsley separately, using pulsing action. As each vegetable is chopped, add to pasta. Add tuna.

3. In food processor (no need to wash it after chopping vegetables), combine mayonnaise, oil and lemon juice. Process until well mixed. Stir in pickle relish, if using.

4. Pour mayonnaise mixture over pasta. Mix well. Season generously with pepper and a little salt, if needed. Salad is best served immediately but can be held for several hours, covered, in refrigerator.

Makes 4 to 6 servings.

482 CALORIES PER SERVING: 23 G PROTEIN; 6 G FAT; 82 G CARBOHYDRATE; 545 MG SODIUM; 18 MG CHOLESTEROL.

Smoked Fish Pasta Salad With Blue Cheese Dressing

Bold flavors make this composed salad memorable. It looks smashing on a buffet table and makes a lovely first course.

¾   pound fettuccine (plain, spinach or combination)
1   tablespoon olive oil
1   cup nonfat plain yogurt
1   cup buttermilk
¼   cup chopped chives or scallions
     Juice of 1 lemon
1   ounce blue cheese, crumbled
     Salt and freshly ground black pepper to taste
1   bunch watercress (about 4 ounces), large stems removed
2   ripe tomatoes, cored, halved and sliced
⅓   pound smoked fish fillet, flaked (about ¾ pound whole fish with bones and skin)
1   small red onion, sliced
1   tablespoon capers, drained

1. Cook pasta in large pot of boiling salted water until just done. Drain and rinse thoroughly to cool. Place in large mixing bowl and toss with olive oil.

2. Combine yogurt, buttermilk, chives or scallions and lemon juice in blender and process to mix. Mix in blue cheese with a rubber spatula.

3. Just before serving, toss pasta with dressing. Season generously with salt and pepper. To serve, arrange watercress on large platter or on oversized salad plates. Mound pasta in center. Arrange tomatoes in overlapping ring around base of pasta. Arrange smoked fish on top of pasta. Sprinkle with onion slices and capers. Grind more pepper on top and serve.

Makes 8 to 10 servings.

259 CALORIES PER SERVING: 14 G PROTEIN; 4 G FAT; 41 G CARBOHYDRATE; 326 MG SODIUM; 10 MG CHOLESTEROL.

Smoked Salmon Pasta Salad

1   pound farfalle, radiatore or other medium-size pasta
2   tablespoons extra-virgin olive oil
6   ounces high-quality smoked salmon, cut into thin strips
1   cucumber, peeled, seeded and sliced
½   red bell pepper, cored, seeded and diced
1   cup frozen peas
4   scallions, trimmed and chopped
¼   cup chopped fresh dill
    Juice of 2 lemons
    Salt and freshly ground black pepper to taste

1. Cook pasta in large pot of boiling salted water until just done. Drain and rinse thoroughly to cool. Place in large mixing bowl and toss with olive oil.

2. Add remaining ingredients and toss again. Add salt and pepper to taste. This salad is best served immediately, though it will keep for several hours refrigerated. To serve, return to room temperature and brighten flavors, if necessary, with additional lemon juice. If desired, garnish with more dill and/or caviar.

Makes 4 to 6 servings.

598 CALORIES PER SERVING: 25 G PROTEIN; 11 G FAT; 98 G CARBOHYDRATE; 374 MG SODIUM; 10 MG CHOLESTEROL.

This makes a special meal, along with hearty rye or pumpernickel bread. It holds up well on a buffet table, especially for Sunday brunch. If you are feeling extravagant, garnish with caviar.

Dilled Smoked Fish Pasta Salad

Any smoked fish will work in this salad, but if you can, choose a smoked fish fillet because it can be handled most easily. If you must buy whole smoked trout or whitefish, make sure you allow for the extra weight of the skin and bones.

¾ pound shells or cavatelli
1 tablespoon olive oil
½ pound smoked fish fillet, flaked (about 1 pound whole smoked fish with skin and bones)
1 cucumber, peeled, seeded and sliced
1 pint cherry tomatoes, quartered or halved
4 thin slices red onion, quartered
¾ cup thinly sliced radishes
¼ cup chopped fresh dill
1 cup buttermilk
Juice of 1 lemon
Salt and freshly ground black pepper to taste

1. Cook pasta in large pot of boiling salted water until just done. Drain and rinse thoroughly to cool. Place in large mixing bowl and toss with olive oil.

2. Combine remaining ingredients with pasta and toss again. Season with salt and pepper. This salad is best served immediately, but it will keep for several hours in the refrigerator. Just before serving, return to room temperature and refresh with additional buttermilk and lemon juice, if desired.

Makes 4 to 6 servings.

472 CALORIES PER SERVING: 27 G PROTEIN; 7 G FAT; 75 G CARBOHYDRATE; 659 MG SODIUM; 21 MG CHOLESTEROL.

Chicken and Turkey
Pasta Salads

Tropical Chicken Pasta Salad

When you are in the mood for something a little exotic, try this combination of chicken and pasta flavored with lime, pineapple, ginger and cilantro.

SALAD

¾   pound radiatore or shells
      Juice of 1 lime (3 tablespoons)
1   tablespoon peanut oil
1   tablespoon reduced-sodium soy sauce
1   large clove garlic
1   1-inch piece peeled ginger
½   chicken breast (about ½ pound)
1   green bell pepper, cored, seeded and finely diced
1   carrot, trimmed, peeled and grated
1   can (16 ounces) crushed pineapple in unsweetened pineapple
      juice, drained, ¼ cup liquid reserved

CILANTRO MAYONNAISE

¼   cup juice from canned pineapple
      Juice of 2 limes (6 tablespoons)
½   cup fat-free mayonnaise
1   tablespoon peanut oil
½   cup chopped fresh cilantro

      Salt and freshly ground black pepper to taste

1. Preheat grill or broiler. Prepare Salad: Cook pasta in large pot of boiling salted water until just done. Drain and rinse thoroughly to cool. Transfer to large mixing bowl.

2. In blender, combine lime juice, peanut oil, soy sauce, garlic and ginger. Blend until smooth. Pour over chicken breasts. Grill or broil for 6 to 8 minutes per side, basting once or twice with marinade, until meat feels firm and looks white throughout. Remove from grill and dice. Add chicken, green pepper, carrot and pineapple to pasta. Toss.

3. Prepare Mayonnaise: Combine reserved pineapple juice, lime juice, mayonnaise, oil and cilantro in blender and blend until creamy-smooth.

(continued on page 72)

71

4. Pour dressing over salad; season to taste with salt and pepper. Serve at once or hold in refrigerator for a few hours. Leftovers can be refreshed with additional lime or pineapple juice.

Makes 4 to 6 servings.

547 CALORIES PER SERVING: 21 G PROTEIN; 9 G FAT; 95 G CARBOHYDRATE; 386 MG SODIUM; 23 MG CHOLESTEROL.

Chicken Pasta Salad

½	pound bowties or other small pasta
2	tablespoons extra-virgin olive oil
1	boneless, skinless chicken breast
2	cloves garlic
2	tablespoons white wine
1	stalk celery, diced
1	carrot, trimmed, peeled and grated
½	green bell pepper, cored, seeded and diced
1	scallion, trimmed and chopped
½	cup fat-free mayonnaise
5	tablespoons fresh lemon juice
1	cup chopped fresh parsley
2	tablespoons chopped fresh dill
1	cup green or red seedless grapes, halved if large
⅓	cup chopped walnuts
	Salt and freshly ground black pepper to taste

1. Cook pasta in large pot of boiling salted water until just done. Drain and rinse thoroughly to cool. Place in large mixing bowl and toss with 1 tablespoon oil.

2. While pasta is cooking, poach chicken: Bring water (enough to cover chicken) to boil with garlic and wine. Poach chicken in barely simmering liquid for about 15 minutes. Remove from poaching liquid and let cool. Add celery, carrot, pepper and scallions to pasta.

3. Combine mayonnaise, lemon juice, remaining 1 tablespoon oil, parsley and dill in food processor or blender and process until smooth.

4. Dice chicken and add to pasta. Pour dressing over and mix well. Mix in grapes and walnuts. Add salt and pepper to taste. If you are not serving immediately, refrigerate, covered. Taste again before serving, adding more lemon juice or salt, if necessary. If desired, garnish with a few extra grapes and walnut pieces.

Makes 4 to 6 servings.

481 CALORIES PER SERVING: 24 G PROTEIN; 16 G FAT; 61 G CARBOHYDRATE; 286 MG SODIUM; 37 MG CHOLESTEROL.

Chicken-Artichoke Pasta Salad With Tomato Dressing

Fresh basil and ripe red tomatoes dominate in this delicious summery salad.

BASIL-TOMATO DRESSING

3	large ripe tomatoes, cored and finely chopped
¼	cup chopped fresh basil
½	cup chopped fresh parsley
3	cloves garlic, finely chopped
3	tablespoons red-wine vinegar
1	tablespoon extra-virgin olive oil
¼	teaspoon salt
	Freshly ground black pepper to taste

SALAD

1	pound orzo
1	tablespoon extra-virgin olive oil
1	boneless, skinless chicken breast
14–16	ounces canned or frozen and defrosted artichoke hearts
	Salt and freshly ground black pepper to taste
	Sprigs of fresh basil for garnish

1. Prepare Dressing: Combine all ingredients in a large salad bowl and set aside.

2. Prepare Salad: Cook orzo in large pot of boiling salted water until just done. Drain and rinse thoroughly to cool. Place in large mixing bowl and toss with olive oil.

3. While pasta cooks, place chicken in boiling water to cover and poach in barely simmering water for about 15 minutes. Remove from water and cut into cubes.

4. Rinse artichoke hearts and cut into quarters. Add orzo, chicken and artichokes to dressing. Toss well. Taste and add salt and pepper, if needed. To serve, garnish with fresh basil sprigs.

Makes 4 to 6 servings.

646 CALORIES PER SERVING: 33 G PROTEIN; 11 G FAT; 105 G CARBOHYDRATE; 407 MG SODIUM; 37 MG CHOLESTEROL.

Autumn Chicken Pasta Salad

The mild flavor of the grape juice in the dressing is echoed in the red grapes. The effect is surprisingly subtle; in fact, no one will guess that grape juice replaces most of the oil in this delectable salad.

GRAPE VINAIGRETTE
½ cup white grape juice
  Juice of 1 lemon
2 tablespoons balsamic vinegar
1 tablespoon chopped fresh oregano or 1 teaspoon dried
½ cup chopped fresh parsley
4 cloves garlic, coarsely chopped
2 tablespoons extra virgin olive oil
  Salt to taste

SALAD
¾ pound twists
1 tablespoon olive oil
1 pound boneless, skinless chicken breast
½ pound green beans, trimmed, cut into 1½-inch lengths
1 cup seedless red grapes, halved if large
1 tart red or green apple, cored and chopped
½ small red onion, chopped

1. Preheat grill or broiler. Prepare Vinaigrette: Combine all ingredients in blender.

2. Prepare Salad: Cook pasta in large pot of boiling salted water. Drain and rinse thoroughly to cool. Place in large mixing bowl and toss with oil.

3. Dab a little dressing on chicken. Grill for 6 to 8 minutes per side. Dice. Blanch green beans in boiling water to cover for 30 seconds. Drain, plunge into ice water to stop cooking and drain again. Add chicken, green beans, grapes, apple and onion to pasta. Toss well. (Salad can be held for several hours by refrigerating in airtight container. Hold dressing at room temperature.)

4. Just before serving, pour remaining dressing over salad. Toss well. Taste and add salt if needed. Transfer to serving bowl.

Makes 4 to 6 servings.

603 CALORIES PER SERVING: 30 G PROTEIN; 14 G FAT; 89 G CARBOHYDRATE; 50 MG SODIUM; 46 MG CHOLESTEROL.

Orzo Turkey Salad

1   pound orzo
3   tablespoons extra-virgin olive oil
1   pound turkey breast cutlets or steaks, cut into 1½-inch cubes
3   tablespoons finely chopped shallots
1   cup defatted chicken broth
2   tablespoons balsamic vinegar
½   red bell pepper, cored, seeded and diced
½   cup frozen peas
2   scallions, trimmed and chopped
2   tablespoons fresh oregano or 2 teaspoons dried
½   cup chopped fresh parsley
     Salt and freshly ground black pepper to taste

1. Cook orzo in large pot of boiling salted water until just done. Drain and rinse thoroughly to cool. Place in large mixing bowl and toss with 1 tablespoon olive oil.

2. Heat remaining 2 tablespoons olive oil in a sauté pan. Add turkey and shallots and sauté for about 5 minutes, until turkey is cooked through. Remove turkey with a slotted spoon and add to orzo.

3. Add chicken broth and vinegar to sauté pan and boil for about 1 minute, stirring constantly to scrape up browned shallots into liquid. Remove from heat.

4. Add pepper, peas, scallions, oregano and parsley to orzo and turkey. Toss well. (Salad can be held for several hours or up to 1 day, by refrigerating pasta and chicken-broth mixture in separate airtight containers.)

5. To serve, pour chicken-broth mixture over salad and toss. Add salt and pepper to taste.

Makes 4 to 6 servings.

688 CALORIES PER SERVING: 39 G PROTEIN; 15 G FAT; 96 G CARBOHYDRATE; 266 MG SODIUM; 50 MG CHOLESTEROL.

This salad is equally delicious made with chicken or turkey, though I prefer turkey. Turkey breast is available as thinly sliced cutlets or more thickly cut steaks. Either may be used since you will cut the meat into bite-size pieces before cooking it.

Smoked Turkey, Pasta and Greens

3	tablespoons extra-virgin olive oil
3	cloves garlic, finely chopped
1	teaspoon chopped fresh herbs (rosemary, basil or oregano)
¾	pound penne
2	tablespoons red-wine vinegar
8	cups salad greens (arugula, cress, endive, radicchio)
3	ripe tomatoes, cored and cut in wedges
¾	pound high-quality smoked turkey breast, cut in ½-inch cubes
	Salt and freshly ground black pepper to taste

1. Heat oil in small skillet. Add garlic and sauté for 1 to 2 minutes. Remove from heat and add herbs. Set aside.

2. Cook pasta in large pot of boiling salted water until just done. Drain and rinse thoroughly to cool. Place in large mixing bowl and toss with 1 tablespoon heated olive oil mixture and set aside.

3. Whisk vinegar into remaining olive oil mixture. Combine greens, tomatoes and turkey with pasta and toss. Pour oil and vinegar over salad and toss well. Season to taste with salt and pepper, if desired. Serve at once.

Makes 4 to 6 servings.

612 CALORIES PER SERVING: 28 G PROTEIN; 22 G FAT; 78 G CARBOHYDRATE; 21 MG SODIUM; 33 MG CHOLESTEROL.

A satisfying salad that can be made with turkey or chicken. The creamy tarragon-mustard dressing is versatile and works well with other combinations, including green salads. Any leftover salad may be refreshed with a little buttermilk mixed with a little more mustard.

Turkey Pasta Salad

SALAD

1	pound small shells or bowties
1	tablespoon olive oil
¾	pound turkey breast cutlets
2	stalks celery, finely chopped
1	red bell pepper, cored, seeded and finely chopped
4	scallions, trimmed and chopped
½	cup chopped fresh parsley

CREAMY TARRAGON-MUSTARD DRESSING

½	cup fat-free mayonnaise
1	cup buttermilk
1	tablespoon olive oil
	Juice of 2 lemons
2	teaspoons Dijon-style mustard
1	tablespoon honey
1	teaspoon dried tarragon

Salt and freshly ground black pepper to taste

1. Preheat grill or broiler. Prepare Salad: Cook pasta in large pot of boiling salted water until just done. Drain and rinse thoroughly to cool. Place in large mixing bowl and toss with oil.

2. While pasta cooks, grill turkey for about 3 minutes per side, until white throughout. Do not overcook. Cut into small cubes. Add to pasta, along with celery, pepper, scallions and parsley. Toss and set aside.

3. Prepare Dressing: Combine all ingredients in blender and process until smooth and creamy. (Salad may be held for several hours, up to 1 day, by refrigerating pasta and dressing in separate airtight containers.)

4. Before serving, allow dressing and salad to return to room temperature, if possible. Remix dressing and pour over salad; toss. Taste and add salt and pepper, if needed.

Makes 4 to 6 servings.

682 CALORIES PER SERVING: 38 G PROTEIN; 11 G FAT; 106 G CARBOHYDRATE; 407 MG SODIUM; 53 MG CHOLESTEROL.

Beef and Pork
Pasta Salads

Thai Beef Salad

1	pound rice vermicelli
½	cup fish sauce
	Juice of 3 limes (6 tablespoons)
¼	cup sugar
1	green chili pepper, chopped
1	carrot, trimmed, peeled and shaved into curls
1	green bell pepper, cored, seeded and cut into thin strips
1	cucumber, peeled, seeded and thinly sliced
¾	pound flank steak, sirloin or other tender cut
1	tablespoon reduced-sodium soy sauce
1	clove garlic, finely chopped
1	green chili pepper, chopped, for garnish (optional)

1. Cook rice vermicelli in large pot of boiling water until tender but still firm, about 5 minutes. Drain and rinse gently. Place in large mixing bowl.

2. Combine fish sauce, lime juice, sugar and strips of chili pepper in small saucepan. Heat until sugar dissolves.

3. Combine carrot, pepper, cucumber and fish sauce mixture with pasta. Toss well. (This can be done up to 1 day before serving.)

4. Just before serving, preheat grill or broiler. Rub beef with soy sauce and garlic. Grill until it reaches desired doneness. A ½-inch-thick steak will take about 3 minutes per side. Slice into thin strips.

5. To serve, place noodles on individual serving plates. Arrange beef on top. Garnish with additional fresh chili pepper, if using.

Makes 4 servings.

580 CALORIES PER SERVING: 30 G PROTEIN; 9 G FAT; 92 G CARBOHYDRATE; 473 MG SODIUM; 64 MG CHOLESTEROL.

Because this salad will hold up well in the refrigerator for at least a day, it is a good choice for a dinner party. Prepare the noodles and vegetables in the morning and grill the steak just before serving.

Warm Noodle Salad With Beef and Beans

1	pound fresh Chinese noodles or ¾ pound linguine
¾	pound London broil or other steak, thinly sliced
1	tablespoon oyster sauce
2	teaspoons reduced-sodium soy sauce
1½	teaspoons chili paste with garlic
3	cloves garlic, finely chopped
1	tablespoon peanut oil
½	pound green beans, trimmed
½	cup defatted chicken broth
4	scallions, trimmed, slivered and cut in 3-inch lengths
12	cherry tomatoes, halved
4–6	cups mixed salad greens

1. Cook noodles in large pot of boiling salted water until just tender. Drain and rinse thoroughly to cool.

2. Combine meat with oyster sauce, soy sauce, chili paste and garlic in medium-size bowl. Heat oil in large wok. Add beef and green beans and stir-fry until meat is just browned, about 2 minutes. Add broth and cover. Steam until beans are tender, about 2 minutes. Remove wok from heat. Stir in noodles, scallions and tomatoes.

3. To serve, arrange greens in large salad bowl or on individual salad plates. Mound warm salad on top. Serve at once.

Makes 4 to 6 servings.

598 CALORIES PER SERVING: 39 G PROTEIN; 11 G FAT; 85 G CARBOHYDRATE; 536 MG SODIUM; 152 MG CHOLESTEROL.

Antipasto Pasta Salad

1   pound ziti, penne or other tubular pasta
2   tablespoons extra-virgin olive oil
¼   pound capocollo, cut into cubes
¼   pound part-skim mozzarella, cut into cubes
2   large tomatoes, cored and chopped
1   small onion, sliced into rings
1   jar (12 ounces) *giardeniera* (mixed pickled vegetables), drained
      and rinsed
1   tablespoon chopped fresh oregano or 1 teaspoon dried
2   tablespoons red-wine vinegar
3   tablespoons defatted chicken broth

1. Cook pasta in large pot of boiling salted water until just done. Drain and rinse thoroughly to cool. Place in large mixing bowl and toss with 1 tablespoon olive oil.

2. In another large mixing bowl, combine capocollo, mozzarella, tomatoes, onion, pickled vegetables and oregano and toss well.

3. In small bowl, combine vinegar and chicken broth. Whisk in remaining 1 tablespoon olive oil. Pour over antipasto mixture and toss. (Salad can be held for a few hours by refrigerating pasta and vegetable mixture in separate airtight containers.)

4. Before serving, return to room temperature and toss together. Serve at once.

Makes 4 to 6 servings.

716 CALORIES PER SERVING: 29 G PROTEIN; 23 G FAT; 97 G CARBOHYDRATE; 893 MG SODIUM; 38 MG CHOLESTEROL.

So named because it contains all the ingredients of a traditional antipasto: pickled vegetables, capocollo, cheese, onions and tomatoes. Capocollo (cured pork shoulder) is available at the delicatessen counter of most supermarkets.

Chinese Barbecued Pork and Noodle Salad

PORK AND MARINADE

2   tablespoons reduced-sodium soy sauce
2   tablespoons sherry
1   tablespoon hoisin sauce
¾   pound boneless pork tenderloin

SALAD

1   pound fresh Chinese noodles or ¾ pound vermicelli
1   tablespoon sesame oil
3   tablespoons hoisin sauce
3   tablespoons reduced-sodium soy sauce
2   tablespoons rice-wine vinegar
1   teaspoon sugar
1   cup fresh snow peas, trimmed (¼ pound)
1   cup bean sprouts
3   large stalks bok choy, sliced
6   scallions, trimmed, slivered lengthwise and cut into
    2-inch pieces

1. Marinate Pork: Combine marinade ingredients in a shallow bowl large enough to hold pork. Add pork and roll in marinade to coat. (Pork can be marinated for up to 8 hours if desired, but it is not necessary. If marinating for more than 30 minutes, refrigerate.)

2. When you are ready to make salad, preheat grill. Cook noodles in large pot of boiling salted water until just done. Drain and rinse thoroughly to cool. Place in large bowl and toss with sesame oil. In small bowl, mix hoisin sauce, soy sauce, rice-wine vinegar and sugar. Add to the pasta and toss.

3. While pasta cooks, briefly blanch snow peas, bean sprouts and bok choy in boiling water to cover for 45 seconds. Immediately plunge into ice water to stop cooking, then drain.

Chinese barbecue sauce, known as hoisin, is the main flavoring agent for this warm salad. It is available wherever Asian foods are sold, as are fresh Chinese noodles and bok choy, a vegetable that resembles a cross between celery and cabbage. The vegetables are briefly blanched to set the color and to cook out the slightly bitter flavor of the raw bean sprouts. To save time, I blanch the vegetables all together.

(continued on page 94)

4. Cook pork on hot grill for 3 to 10 minutes per side, depending on thickness. Pork is done when meat is firm throughout and just barely shows pink. Do not overcook. Cut into matchstick-size pieces. Add vegetables and pork to noodles. Toss to mix well. Serve at once.

Makes 4 to 6 servings.

594 CALORIES PER SERVING: 38 G PROTEIN; 10 G FAT; 84 G CARBOHYDRATE; 834 MG SODIUM; 158 MG CHOLESTEROL.

Index